THE CAT DID NOT MY TONGUE

HI, MY NAME IS ANDREW, AND I AM A VERY HAPPY BOY

ARTUR RAUSHEN

ILLUSTRATED BY
DIRCEU VEIGA

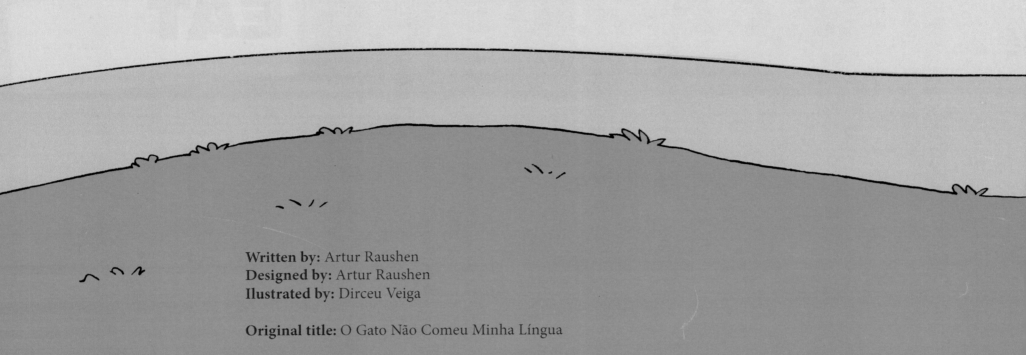

Written by: Artur Raushen
Designed by: Artur Raushen
Ilustrated by: Dirceu Veiga

Original title: O Gato Não Comeu Minha Língua

www.instagram.com/selective.mutism.book

UNTIL ONE DAY WE WERE SITTING IN A CIRCLE...
IT WAS ALMOST MY TURN. MY HEART STARTED TO BEAT FASTER,

BUT I KNEW THE ANSWER.

I TOOK A DEEP BREATH AND...

EVERYTHING HAPPENED IN MY TIME,
STEP BY STEP
WITHOUT PRESSURE.

I BECAME BRAVER AND BRAVER!

I FELT MORE AND MORE COMFORTABLE IN THE SESSIONS.
EVEN WITHOUT MY MOM.

I FELT COMFORTABLE WITH SOME OF MY FRIENDS AND, AT RECESS, I WHISPERED TO THEM.
I FELT REALLY HAPPY WITH MY VICTORY.

WE MADE A CHART OF MY IMPROVEMENTS

I WILL TALK TO	I AM TALKING TO	I ALREADY TALK TO	PLACES I TALKED
JOHN	DAVID	LAUREN	READING ROOM
ALEX	NOAH	EMMA	PARK
CHARLES		MICHAEL	CLASSROOM
ROBERT		JENNIFER	LUNCH ROOM
MARY		SANDY	
		TEACHER	

WE REPEATED THIS PROCEDURE MANY TIMES,
WITH DIFFERENT FRIENDS
AND IN DIFFERENT LOCATIONS.

WE ALSO DID THIS AT HOME WHEN I INVITED
A FRIEND OVER.
AT FIRST, MY MOM HELPED ME
BUT AFTERWARDS I WAS ABLE TO TALK ALONE
TO MY FRIEND.

THE FOLLOWING WEEK, MY MOM STARTED TO GO WITH ME TO SCHOOL BEFORE CLASS TIME,
THE TWO OF US WOULD GO TO A DIFFERENT CLASSROOM TO TALK, PLAY AND HAVE FUN.

TIPS OF GAMES:

- UNO©
- CARD GAMES
- COUNTING NUMBERS
- DICE

IN THE BEGINNING, I DID NOT SAY ANYTHING, BUT SLOWLY I FELT MORE COMFORTABLE
UNTIL I WAS ABLE TO SPEAK...   I EVEN GOT CANDY!

ONLY AFTER TRAINING A LOT IS WHEN WE ARE ABLE TO GO DOWN A SLOPE. SWIMMING IS ALSO LIKE THIS.

I LEARNED THAT I NEED TO IMPROVE SLOWLY,
AT MY OWN PACE, MY WAY, LIKE EVERYTHING IN LIFE.
FOR EXAMPLE, RIDING A BIKE NEEDS LOTS OF PRACTICE.
FIRST USING TRAINING WHEELS AND ONLY IN A FLAT PLACE.

HE SAID THAT HE MET MANY KIDS LIKE ME AND HAS HELPED ALL OF THEM TO OVERCOME THEIR ISSUES.
FIRST HE TAUGHT ME HOW TO RELAX, BREATHING DEEPLY AND COUNTING FROM 1 TO 10.

TODAY I AM GOING TO MEET SOMEONE WHO SAYS THAT THEY ARE GOING TO HELP ME.

THE WORST PART IS WHEN WE ARE IN A CIRCLE AND THE TEACHER ASKS EACH AND EVERY STUDENT TO ANSWER. I KNOW THAT MY TURN IS COMING, AND AS MUCH AS I WOULD LIKE TOO, NOT A SINGLE SOUND COMES OUT.

AT HOME, I TALK NORMALLY, SOMETIMES EVEN TOO MUCH.

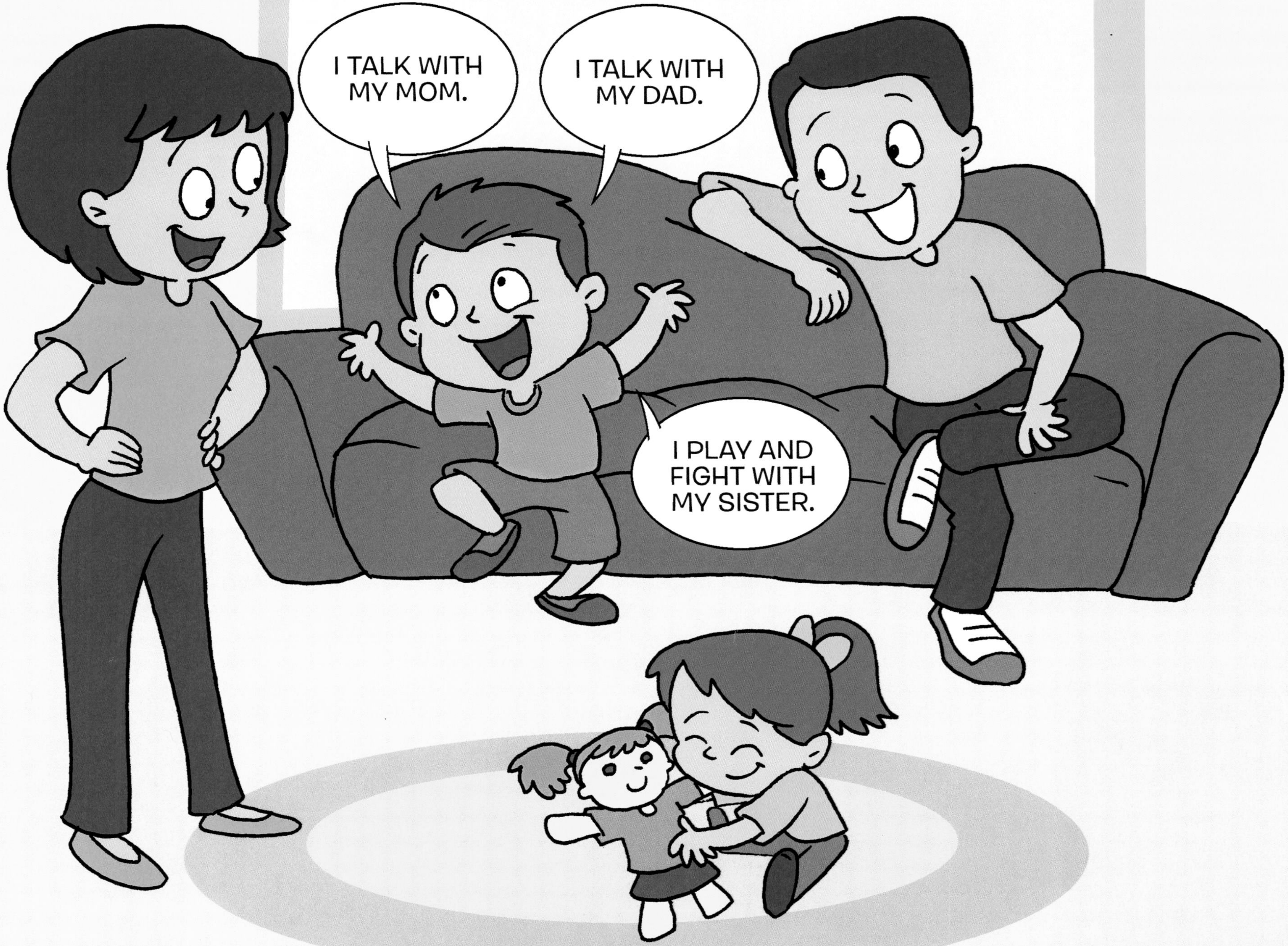

To parents:

Selective mutism is an anxiety disorder most prominent in children although it may affect them also during adulthood. Patients are unable to speak in certain places and to specific people, but are able to speak normally at home with their parents and siblings.

Selective mutism affects about 7 out of every 1,000 children. Due to a lack of literature and knowledge, many children do not have their diagnosis recognized, delaying and aggravating the condition.

This book serves as an introduction to the child's treatment technique called Stimulus fading, known to be an effective technique for treating selective mutism.

Having knowledge on how this technique will be performed, the child better understands the treatment. This reduces anxiety and creates an environment in which the child may overcome selective mutism.

CPSIA information can be obtained
at www.ICGtesting.com
Printed in the USA
BVRC100806240222
629774BV00023B/43